WORLD'S WORST...

OIL

Disasters

Rob Alcraft

Heinemann Library
Chicago, Illinois

© 2000 Reed Educational & Professional Publishing
Published by Heinemann Library
an imprint of Reed Educational & Professional Publishing,
100 N. LaSalle, Suite 1010
Chicago, IL 60602

Customer Service 888-454-2279

Designed by Celia Floyd
Illustrations by David Cuzik (Pennant Illustration) and Jeff Edwards
Originated by Dot Gradations
Printed by Wing King Tong, in Hong Kong

04 03 02 01 00
10 9 8 7 6 5 4 3 2 1

Library of Congress Cataloging-in-Publication Data
Alcraft, Rob, 1966-
    Oil disasters / Rob Alcraft.
        p. cm. – (World's worst)
    Included bibliographical references and index.
    Summary: Examines three of the world's worst man-made
oil disasters, discussing the consequences and how they could have been
averted.
    ISBN 1-57572-990-3 (library binding)
    1. Oil spills—Environmental aspects Juvenile literature. 2. Oil
wells--Fires and fire prevention—Environmental aspects Juvenile
literature. 3. Petroleum industry and trade—Safety measures
Juvenile literature. [1. Oil spills 2. Water—Pollution.
3. Pollution.] I. Title. II. Series.
TD196.P4A44 1999
363.738'2—dc21   99-27878
                                                            CIP

Acknowledgments
The Publishers would like to thank the following for permission to reproduce photographs:
Still Pictures/Bob Evans, p. 4; Ecoscene/Sally Morgan, p. 5; Still Pictures/Pierre Gleizes, p. 6;
Oxford Scientific Films/Richard Packwood, p. 7; P. Nicol, p. 9; ITN, p. 12; Today p. 13; Black
Star/Charles Mason, p. 14; Still Pictures/Dominique Halleux, p. 15; Science Photo Library/
Vanessa Vick, p. 18; Still Pictures, p. 19; Oxford Scientific Films/Michael McKinnon, p. 20; Still
Pictures/Brent Occlesham, p. 21; Sygma/S-Compoint, p. 24; Planet Earth Pictures/Doug Perrine,
p. 25; Geoffrey Bollands/Today p. 26; Ann Ronan Picture Library p. 27; Rex Features, p. 29.

Cover photograph reproduced with permission of Steve McCurry/Magnum Photos.

Any words appearing in the text in bold, **like this**, are explained in the glossary

Contents

The Oil Industry

We use oil in everything from ink to explosives. Oil runs our cars and fuels our factories. We all depend on it. And because we all need it, oil is very precious. Oil means money. Countries that have a lot of oil are often very rich.

Finding, selling, and **refining** oil is one of the world's biggest industries. Companies drill for oil in the frozen lands of Siberia and in the hot, dry deserts of the Middle East. Amazing technologies have been made that can even pump oil from hundreds of feet below the sea.

This offshore **oil rig** in the Santa Barbara Channel in California brings up oil from beneath the seabed.

All over the world, governments make laws to prevent accidents and disasters in the oil industry. Companies are expected to make sure that their businesses are safe and do not pose a threat to people or the **environment**. Yet oil is a world business. Millions of people are involved. Somewhere, sometime, something will always go wrong.

Where does oil come from?

Oil is the remains of tiny plants and animals that lived in the sea millions of years ago. When these living things died, they sank to the bottom. They were covered by mud and sand. Over millions of years, weight and heat and tiny **bacteria** changed the animals and plants into oil. Today, oil is found in soft, spongy rocks— usually trapped deep beneath a layer of hard rock.

Oil for dinner!

When oil comes out of the ground, it is thick and usually black. This thick black oil is called crude oil. First it is refined. Refining is a little like cooking. It separates the oil into its many different parts.

These different oil parts are made into thousands of different things besides gasoline to run cars. For instance, you wear oil in clothes made from nylon. Oil is used in fabric dye. You paint oil on your face in make-up. Oil is used in fertilizer for growing food and in medicines to make you better. Oil is used in car tires, plastics, and **pesticides**. You even eat oil, added to your food as color and **preservative**!

This sticky black substance is crude oil. The world's biggest producer of crude oil is Russia.

When Things Go Wrong

The oil business is dangerous. Oil is often found in places that are difficult to get to and difficult to work in. There is a constant risk of accidents as people fly to and from **oil rigs**. In deserts—where it is very hot or very cold—machines don't always work well. People find it hard to concentrate.

Oil burns easily. Also, it often contains, or is found with, gas. A tiny spark can cause fires and explosions. Underground oil is under **pressure**—just like a shaken can of cola. If **valves** and pipes in **oil wells** crack or burst, oil and gas roar out. **Capping**, or stopping, an oil well can be difficult and dangerous. In March 1992, oil found in Uzbekistan was under so much pressure that wells drilled into it could not be controlled. The wells broke, and oil gushed hundreds of feet into the air for 62 days.

Following the Persian Gulf War in 1991, entire oil fields were on fire, with billions of gallons of oil blazing out of control.

Oil pollution turns this beach in South Devon, England, black and sticky.

Many oil spills and fires are small. No one is killed. The **environment** recovers from the poisonous oil. But sometimes accidents are serious.

In this book we look at three of the worst disasters to hit the oil business —and the world—in the twentieth century. We look at the stories of those who were there and who survived. We look at what went wrong and why disaster struck. Is there something about oil that will always spell disaster?

Everyday disaster

Most oil **pollution** isn't caused by single disasters. It is caused by small oil spills and leaks from ships. Around the world, two and half times more pollution is caused by ordinary shipping than by dramatic tanker or oil rig accidents. Even if a tanker hasn't run aground on your favorite beach, you may still find patches of thick tarry oil.

Blow Out!
The Piper Alpha Oil Rig Disaster

On July 6, 1988, the Piper Alpha **oil rig** off the east coast of Scotland exploded in flames. 167 men were killed. It was the worst disaster ever to hit Scotland's oil industry.

Piper Alpha
Scotland

Fireball

The Piper Alpha oil rig stood on four giant legs, 304 feet (92 meters) high. It was home to over 200 workers.

Piper Alpha was used to drill for oil. From deep beneath the seabed, the oil was piped to shore. But where there is oil, there is also gas. On Piper Alpha, some gas was pumped to land, while some was burned off in a giant flare.

On July 4, men on Piper Alpha said there was a strange smell from the gas on the rig. Something wasn't quite right. Then on July 6, an engineer removed a **valve** in the gas pumping system so that it could be checked and repaired. Investigation after the disaster found that he didn't put the valve back.

Bill Lobban survived the Piper Alpha disaster. This is his story, which appeared in the *Times* newspaper on July 7, 1988.

There were a lot of flames and smoke and gradually it came into the accommodation section but we managed to find our way out onto the pipe deck.

There were more explosions and the rig tilted to an angle of 30 degrees. It just suddenly dropped down at one side and the explosions continued around us.

It was just terrifying. I ran out when there was a lull in the flames and smoke. We knew this was our one chance. We could touch nothing on deck because it was burning red hot. So we just ran to the edge and jumped straight into the water. Flames were shooting 70 or 100 meters into the air.

This photograph of fire engulfing the Piper Alpha oil rig appeared on the front pages of many newspapers the day after the disaster.

When the shift changed, the engineer who had removed the valve went to rest. Other men came on duty. It was night. The sea lifted and surged 100 feet (30 meters) below. Hours went by.

Then at 9:45 P.M., the burning gas flare began to roar. Five minutes later, a gas pump failed. Gas leaked and then **ignited**. Piper Alpha exploded in flames.

Escape from the Inferno

As the Piper Alpha **oil rig** burned, there was confusion and shouting. Men climbed out onto the structure of the rig to escape the fire. Some jumped out into the darkness—a 100-foot (30-meter) jump into freezing seas.

On the rig, explosions destroyed fire-fighting equipment. The men could do little to fight the fire. They could only try to escape or wait for help. The Piper Alpha rig was burning out of control.

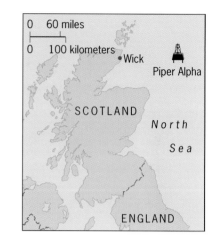

1. At 9:58 P.M., an explosion rips through the Piper Alpha oil rig. Equipment meant to shut down the flow of oil from beneath the sea is blown away. Oil and gas spew into the flames, fueling the fire, and causing explosion after explosion. Survivors talk of more than 20 explosions.

2. The first **SOS** message is received at Wick, 96 miles (160 kilometers) away. It is 10:01 P.M. The search for survivors begins.

3. At the time of the first explosion, divers are working beneath the rig. As a safety measure, automatic fire equipment—supposed to drench the rig with water—has been turned off. There is no way of fighting the fire on Piper Alpha.

4. Men are trapped in the sleeping quarters. This room stands directly above the oil and gas of the main drilling area. The men have been trained to wait for helicopters to **evacuate** them— but the landing pad is destroyed.

5. Beneath the rig, a boat called the *Sandhaven* tries to rescue men in the water. But at 10:22 P.M., a second massive explosion engulfs the rig and the ship in a fireball. On the ship's deck, three men are killed. A rescue boat is destroyed in the water. Even the sea is burning.

6. The hospital ship *Tharos* treats injured men. Helicopters ferry survivors to the hospital ship and to the shore.

7. By morning, little of the rig remains above water. The structure is tilting. Oil and gas shoot flames and smoke into the air. Red Adair, an oil firefighter, is called in to **cap** the wells and put out the fires. But bad weather delays action. Six days later, two wells on the rig are still burning.

The Cold Light of Day

The Piper Alpha **oil rig** burned for over a week before firefighters were able to **cap** the wells.

The Piper Alpha disaster began one of the largest emergency operations ever in the North Sea. At least 12 ships and 6 helicopters were sent to help rescuers. By 3:00 A.M., 40 people had been lifted from the sea, but 167 men had died.

How did it happen?

In 1997, a court in Scotland blamed two men—Terence Sutton and Robert Vernon—for the disaster. They were the engineers responsible for the missing **valve** in the gas pumping system. But oil worker **unions** and relatives of the men were angry. The two men had been killed during the disaster and could not answer the charges. The evidence was all at the bottom of the sea. How could anyone really know what had gone wrong? Ann Gillanders, from the Piper Alpha Families and Survivors Association, said the court was wrong. She said, "The management was deficient as far as safety was concerned, and the buck stops at the top." She pointed to the long record of fires and accidents on oil rigs in the North Sea.

There had been 32 serious accidents on rigs in 1987, and 72 the year before. It was not a good safety record.

Safety experts and many men who had worked on Piper Alpha said the rig was dangerous. The sleeping quarters, where 122 men died, were right on top of the most explosive and dangerous area on the rig. Safety alarms were also often ignored. The rig was rusting and unstable. Allan Millar of the Professional Diver Association said, "That rig had quite a reputation. It was felt that if anything did happen it would be on that particular platform."

Changing the laws

After the disastrous fire on the Piper Alpha oil rig, the British government made changes to some of the safety laws. Today, by law, everyone on an oil platform has a survival suit, a life jacket, and other special protective clothing. Everyone on a rig also has to have special training so they know what to do in an emergency. Rigs also have to have quick escape routes to lifeboats.

The Piper Alpha tragedy brought misery to many families.

Wreck!
The Exxon Valdez Oil Disaster

On March 25, 1989, the **supertanker** *Exxon Valdez* smashed into Bligh **Reef** off the Alaskan coast. Its 30,000-ton cargo of oil spewed into the sea. A 90-mile (150-kilometer) **oil slick** spread from the tanker. It was the worst oil spill in American history.

Heading into disaster

At 9:00 P.M., the *Exxon Valdez* edged its way from port, and headed out into Alaska's Prince William Sound. The weather was good and the seas were calm. At 11:30 P.M., the U.S. Coast Guard received a call over the radio. The *Exxon Valdez* wanted permission to steer east, to avoid icebergs up ahead. Permission was given.

At midnight, the captain set the new course and went to his cabin. He left the ship's third mate in charge. He told him to steer back into the normal shipping lane in a few minutes, when the danger was past. He didn't tell him the ship was on **autopilot**.

Oil was pumped from the wreck of the *Exxon Valdez* into rescue tankers.

The third mate changed the course back to the shipping lane, or so he thought. Eleven minutes passed. The giant ship sailed on into the darkness—on the wrong course. Suddenly the rocks of Bligh Reef loomed up on the **radar**. But by now it was too late. The *Exxon Valdez* plowed into the reef, punching eight gaping holes in the tanker's **starboard** side. Two of its 13 giant tanks were punctured. Then the tanker smashed into the main body of Bligh Reef. Six more tanks were gashed open. Oil spilled from its ruptured tanks. The *Exxon Valdez* had struck disaster.

This is the story of the disaster as witnessed by James Kunkel, chief mate of the *Exxon Valdez*.

I feared for my life. I wondered if we were going to see the sunrise.

*There was so much **hull** damage. The reef below was being ground to tiny pieces. The ship was unstable. It could have come off the rocks at any time.*

It still had more than 42 million gallons [190 million liters] of oil on board, and we didn't want to spill any more. It was in danger of sinking. We would have been drowned.

A poisonous slick

For sea life, oil is poison. When birds try to clean oil from their feathers, they swallow large amounts of it. When the fur of seals and otters becomes clogged with oil, they cannot float or keep warm. They sink and die. The 90-mile (150-kilometer) oil slick from the *Exxon Valdez* proved to be deadly. It **contaminated** 1,200 miles (2,000 kilometers) of coastline. Wherever the oil touched the shore, the sea **environment** began to die.

The Clean-up Begins

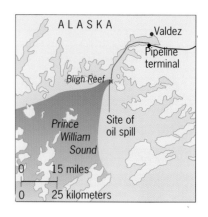

As the *Exxon Valdez* lay stranded on the rocks, emergency action should have begun. But for 12 hours, nothing happened. The ship's owners and the local government couldn't agree on what to do. The weather turned bad. Storms churned the **oil slick** into a thick sludge, which washed out into the sea.

The *Exxon Valdez* did not sink. No one died. Even so, the oil slick became an **environmental** disaster. Cleaning it up took many months and cost $2.5 billion. 10,000 people were involved. No one knew if the seas and beaches could ever fully recover.

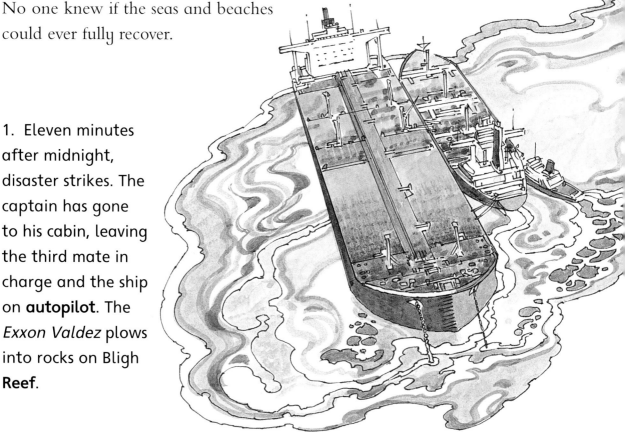

1. Eleven minutes after midnight, disaster strikes. The captain has gone to his cabin, leaving the third mate in charge and the ship on **autopilot**. The *Exxon Valdez* plows into rocks on Bligh **Reef**.

2. Oil is pumped from the ship into rescue tankers. Workers can't pump it out quickly enough. Oil is spilling into the sea at a rate of more than 200,000 gallons (910,000 liters) a minute. Storms push the oil slick out into Prince William Sound.

5. Birds and animals are caught in the thick sludge of oil. Hundreds of thousands die. The fishing industry has to stop work.

4. Clean-up teams work with local **volunteers** to mop up the oil. Boats tow booms to skim the oil off the sea. Hoses, chemicals, and huge mechanical sponges are used to clean rocks on the beaches. But on the next tide, there is more oil brought in by the sea. The slick washes over 1,200 miles (2,000 kilometers) of coastline.

3. Thirty-six hours later, a floating **boom** is placed around the ship to keep oil from spreading. It is too late to hold the oil back. The only way to clean up the oil slick is to scoop it from the sea. Most of it will be impossible to clean up. Equipment stored for just such an emergency is under deep snow. Most of the equipment does not work.

The Cost of Disaster

Scientists still disagree about how much damage the *Exxon Valdez* disaster really did. The spill killed hundreds of thousands of fish, otters, and seabirds. Scientists working for the oil company that owned the ship say that the **environment** has not been damaged forever. Today, the numbers of birds in the area are the same as before the disaster. Fish seem to live and breed without problems.

Other scientists are not convinced that the animal and plant life of Prince William Sound has recovered. The murre, a small, penguin-like bird, no longer breeds. Some baby salmon are hatching malformed or even dead.

Scientists found that cleaning up the oil also did a lot of damage. The hot water hoses and chemicals used to clean the oil from beaches killed important sea plants. The clean-up actually made the beaches worse in some cases.

Oil-eating organisms

Tiny organisms called **bacteria** live everywhere. Each type of bacteria has a favorite food. For instance, some bacteria cause the mold that grows on food or on damp bathroom walls. There are even bacteria that like to eat oil!

After the *Exxon Valdez* disaster, special bacteria were sprayed on patches of oil-covered beach. The tests showed that the bacteria could actually eat the spilled oil that was so poisonous to sea life. In just five months, they could leave beaches almost clean. These bacteria are now being used to help clean up after many oil spills.

Thousands of volunteers helped to clean up the Alaska coast after the *Exxon Valdez* disaster. Hot water hoses were used to remove the oil.

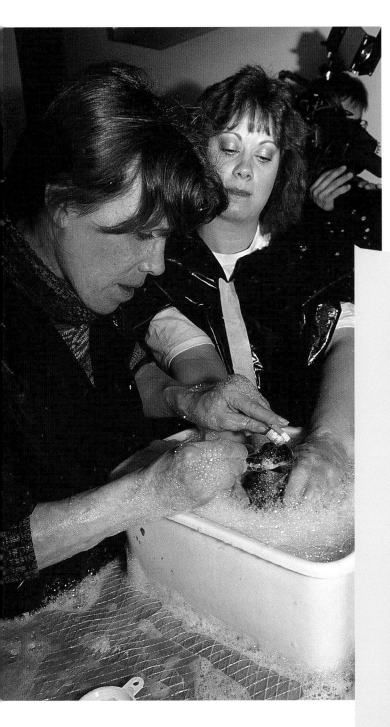

An oil-covered seabird, one of the many victims of the Exxon Valdez oil spill, is being carefully cleaned using an old toothbrush.

Disaster brings new laws

The *Exxon Valdez* disaster, and public reaction to it, meant that the government was forced to take action. It passed the Oil **Pollution** Act in 1990. This law put tougher penalties on companies responsible for oil spills. Tanker owners and oil companies must now make emergency plans in case of accidents. All tankers using U.S. waters are required to have double **hulls,** so there is less chance they will sink or leak oil. A special "spill fund" has also been set up—paid for by a tax on each barrel of oil. People in areas affected by oil spills can use money from this fund.

Oil War!
The Gulf War Oil Spills

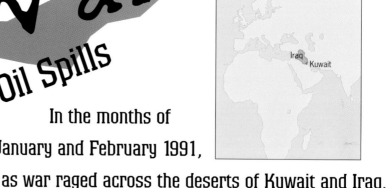

In the months of January and February 1991, as war raged across the deserts of Kuwait and Iraq, retreating soldiers began a campaign of **sabotage**. They blew up hundreds of **oil wells** and began emptying oil into the sea. It threatened to be one of the worst **environmental** disasters the world had ever seen.

When the sky turned black

When Iraq invaded Kuwait, the Gulf War began. Kuwait had some of the largest **oil fields** in the world. Iraq wanted control over this oil. An international military force attacked the Iraqi army and forced them to retreat. But as Iraqi soldiers left Kuwait, they blew up oil wells.

By the end of February 1991, over 730 oil wells were turned into towers of flame. Thick, oily smoke shot into the air, filling the skies of Kuwait black with **toxic** smoke. The cloud of smoke climbed over 2.4 miles (4 kilometers) high. Experts predicted that the fires could burn for years.

The burning oil wells blocked out the sun and turned the day as cold as night.

A seemingly endless flow of oil gushes from sabotaged and war-damaged oil pipes.

Iraqi soldiers also dumped oil from tankers and stores on the coast. Other oil spewed from war-damaged storage tanks and oil pipelines bombed by the attacking forces. A massive **oil slick** formed and spread slowly across the clear blue waters of the Persian Gulf. Over 6 million barrels of oil spilled into the sea. The slick covered 370 square miles (960 square kilometers) of sea. It covered beaches and rocks, killing birds, fish, and sea life.

Hammad Butti, an oil worker from Kuwait, saw and heard the sabotage of the oil fields. This interview appeared in the *National Geographic* magazine in August 1991.

*On Sunday, February 17, they began to fire the wells. They put dynamite in each, put a sandbag on each **charge** to direct the blast downward, and **detonated** it with an electric charge. Every 10 or 15 minutes they fired another well—boom! Soon the sky was full of fire and smoke.*

21

The Legacy of a War

At the end of the Gulf War, much of Kuwait was in ruins. Over 100,000 soldiers and **civilians** from all sides had been killed. Lakes of oil covered miles of Kuwaiti desert. Dynamited **oil wells** burned fiercely. The capital city was ghostly quiet and dark under a blanket of thick, black smoke.

1. In August 1990, Kuwait is **invaded** and occupied by Iraq. In January and February 1991, Iraqi troops are forced to retreat. Soldiers begin to **sabotage** Kuwait's oil industry, blowing up oil wells and dumping stored oil into the sea.

2. The huge Mina al-Ahmadi oil **refinery** is emptied. Between 6 and 8 million barrels of oil flood into the Persian Gulf. There is massive **pollution**. An **oil slick** floats south with the currents, covering 288 miles (480 kilometers) of beaches. Between one and two million birds are killed by the oil. Fish and sea animals die, and delicate corals and coastal plants are devastated.

3. By February 1991, 732 oil wells burn out of control. Some fires shoot 198 feet (60 meters) into the air. The smoke and pollution drift 1,440 miles (2,400 kilometers) into northern India, where the oil blackens the snow. Other wells gush oil, forming poisonous black lakes, some more than 1 mile (1.5 kilometers) long.

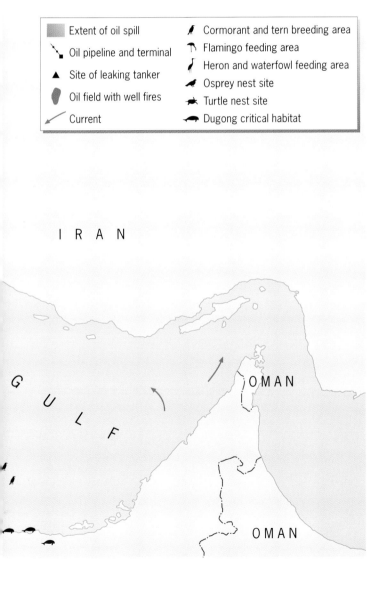

▨ Extent of oil spill	🐦 Cormorant and tern breeding area
↘ Oil pipeline and terminal	🦩 Flamingo feeding area
▲ Site of leaking tanker	🦆 Heron and waterfowl feeding area
▮ Oil field with well fires	🦅 Osprey nest site
↗ Current	🐢 Turtle nest site
	🦭 Dugong critical habitat

I R A N

G
U
L
F

OMAN

OMAN

4. It takes until November to **cap** the last burning oil well. Then the clean up begins. Oil is scraped from beaches and bays. Almost 1.4 million barrels of oil are collected and dumped in pits. The job is made more difficult and dangerous by the **land mines** and bombs left from the war.

Damaged Seas

An **environmental** study six months after the disaster in the Gulf reported that the effects had been "tragic." A study by the International Atomic Energy Agency's marine experts was carried out from June to October 1991. Experts found that severe oil **pollution** was restricted to the Saudi Arabian coastline within about 240 miles (400 kilometers) of the spillages.

Marine experts found less pollution than normal in some areas of the Gulf. This was because the war had stopped the normal trade in oil, which spills around 2 million barrels of oil into the Persian Gulf every year.

Oil workers struggle to cap a gushing oil well in Kuwait.

There is no doubt that the oil spills hurt Kuwait. On some beaches, oil and sand mixed to form a tar-like surface 12 inches (30 centimeters) thick. Oil experts also worked out that it takes the Persian Gulf at least five years to flush out polluted water through the narrow channel that connects it to the world's oceans. Many experts say it will take many years to heal the damage.

Stopping the fires

Stopping—or **capping**—an **oil well** is dangerous work. Once the fire is out, a giant plug has to be jammed into the well, and mud pumped in to stop the well for good. In Kuwait, there was the added danger of **land mines** left from the war. Mines often had to be cleared before firefighters and oil well experts could start work.

Wildlife in danger

The Persian Gulf abounds with sea life. Its shallow, warm waters are a perfect home for shrimps, oysters, and coral. There are turtles, flamingos, and dugongs. The rare dugong was one of the animals most at risk in the oil spill. Even before the Gulf War, scientists thought the dugong would be wiped out by oil pollution. The oil disaster in the Gulf has made the dugong's fight for survival even more difficult.

The dugong, a large gentle mammal similar to the manatee, was at great risk from the oil pollution.

Oil and Safety

Most disasters are preventable. The Disaster Prevention Unit at Bradford University in England studied over 1,000 disasters. It showed that six in every ten could have been avoided. This is true for the oil disasters in this book. Perhaps only the Gulf War disaster was difficult to prevent. It is very difficult to stop an army that decides to **sabotage** an **oil field**.

A Piper Alpha survivor can go home at last.

Alternatively, the Piper Alpha disaster showed that important safety lessons should have already been learned from other North Sea accidents. For instance, experts had already agreed that it was not a good idea to have men living over a part of an **oil rig** that could explode. If Piper Alpha had been built differently, many lives might have been saved.

In the *Exxon Valdez* disaster, better emergency equipment would have stopped much of the oil spill from spreading. If people in charge had acted quickly, the giant **oil slick** might never have washed out into the sea.

Sometimes, safety precautions are not taken because of money. People in the oil industry have to make a profit to stay in business. They do not want to spend money until they know safety measures are going work. And more safety means more cost. How much more would we be willing to pay for oil and all the things that come from it, such as heating or car travel?

A history of oil

People have known about oil for thousands of years. They burned it for light, and they used it for waterproofing. In the 1850s, kerosene was distilled for the first time from oil and used as cheap fuel for lamps.

The first **oil wells** were sunk in Germany in 1857. The first American oil well was sunk in Pennsylvania in 1859. When the gasoline engine was invented, and cars became more common after World War I, the oil industry became an essential part of the modern world.

In 1905, these oil **derricks** were built over what had been a residential area of Los Angeles, California.

The World's Worst Oil Disasters

Torrey Canyon, England, March 18, 1967 An oil tanker hits rocks off Cornwall. 120,000 tons of oil wash into the sea.

Amoco Cadiz, France, March 1978 An oil tanker breaks up off the French coast and spills 220,000 tons of oil.

Ixtoc oil rig, Mexico, June 3, 1979 An oil rig blow-out in the Gulf of Mexico spills 500,000 tons of oil into the sea.

Atlantic Empress and *Aegean Captain*, Caribbean Sea, July 19, 1979 Two tankers collide and spill 280,000 tons of oil.

Piper Alpha, Scotland, July 6, 1988 Oil and gas explode on an oil rig, killing 167 people. The rig is destroyed.

Exxon Valdez, Alaska, March 25, 1989 An oil tanker hits rocks off the Alaskan coast. 30,000 tons of oil wash into the sea.

Gulf War, January–November 1991 **Oil well** and oil storage **sabotage** spills 6 to 8 million barrels of oil and destroys over 730 oil wells.

Fergana Valley, Uzbekistan, March 1992 An oil well blow-out spills over 6 million barrels of oil onto the land around the well. The blow-out lasts 62 days.

The world's oil

This map shows the world's main oil-producing countries. You can also see where the world's worst oil disasters and pollution are.

Major oil producers

Oil spills from Persian Gulf War (1991)

Oil rig blowouts (1967 to early 1990s)

Major tanker spills (1983–93) over 35,000 tons spilled

Oil wells in Libya pump thousands of gallons. Oil is an important industry in the Middle East.

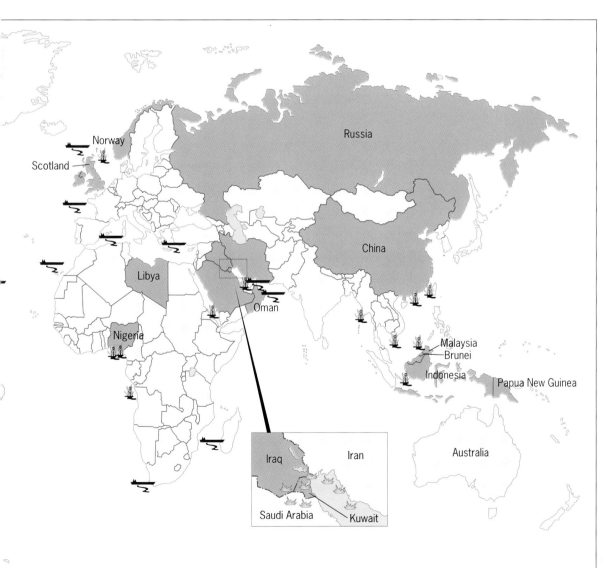

Glossary

autopilot navigation system that allows a plane or ship to steer itself

bacteria one of the simplest and smallest form of life. They live in large numbers in the air, soil, and water.

boom floating barrier used to stop oil slicks from spreading

cap to stop up an oil well

civilian someone not in the armed services

charge small quantity of explosive

contaminated having a dangerous substance on or in it

derrick framework holding the drilling machinery over an oil well

detonated when something is blown up

environment external surroundings; the land, water and air around us

evacuate to move people from a dangerous place

hull body of a boat or ship

ignite set on fire

invade to enter a country by military force, usually with the aim of taking control of that country

land mine explosive mine (bomb) laid on or under the ground

oil field place where there is a lot of oil underground

oil rig metal structure in the middle of the sea used to drill out oil from deep below the seabed

oil slick smooth patch of oil on the sea

oil well deep hole drilled down into the ground to get to oil

pesticide chemical used to kill or control insects

pollution damage to the environment caused by poisonous or harmful substances

preservative something added to food to keep it fresh longer

pressure force of one thing in contact with another

radar way of detecting objects using radio waves

reef ridge of rock just under the surface of the sea

refining separating oil into its many different parts

refinery place where oil is refined

sabotage to damage something on purpose

SOS international code of extreme distress

starboard right-hand side of a boat or ship

supertanker giant and fast ship that can carry a huge cargo

toxic poisonous

union organization which represents groups of workers

valve tap inside a pipe which can be turned off or on

volunteer person who helps without being paid

More Books to Read

Blashfield, Jean, and Wallace Black. *Oil Spills*. Danbury, Conn.: Children's Press, 1991.

Markle, Sandra. *After the Spill: The Exxon Valdez Disaster, Then & Now*. New York: Walker & Company, 1999.

Wright, Russell. *Oil Spill!* Reading, Mass.: Addison Wesley Longman, Inc., 1991.

Index